EMPOWERED BY THE HOLY SPIRIT

EMPOWERED BY THE HOLY SPIRIT

A Study in the Ministries of Worship

Robert E. Webber

The Alleluia! Series of the Institute for Worship Studies

Hendrickson Publishers, Inc.
P. O. Box 3473
Peabody, Massachusetts 01961-3473

EMPOWERED BY THE HOLY SPIRIT:
A Study in the Ministries of Worship
by Robert E. Webber

ISBN 1-56563-273-7

First printing, January 1998

Printed in the United States of America

CONTENTS

WELCOME TO THE ALLELUIA! SERIES

This Bible study series has been designed by the Institute for Worship Studies primarily for laypersons in the church.

We are living in a time when worship has become a distinct priority for the church. For years, the church has emphasized evangelism, teaching, fellowship, missions, and service to society to the neglect of the very source of its power—worship. But in recent years we have witnessed a Spirit-led renewal in the study and practice of worship.

Because worship has been neglected for so many years, there is precious little information and teaching on the subject in our seminaries, Bible schools, and local churches.

The mission of the Institute for Worship Studies is to make the study of worship available to everyone in the church—academician, pastor, worship leader, music minister, and layperson.

Laypersons will find the seven courses of the Alleluia! Series to be inspiring, informative, and life changing. Each course of study is rooted in biblical teaching, draws from the rich historical treasures of the church, and is highly practical and accessible.

The Institute for Worship Studies presents this course, *Empowered by the Holy Spirit: A Study in the Ministries of Worship,* as a service to the local church and to its ministry of worship to God. May this study warm your heart, inform your mind, and kindle your spirit. May it inspire and set on fire the worship of the local church. And may this study minister to the church and to the One, Holy, Triune God in whose name it is offered.

THE SEVEN COURSES IN THE ALLELUIA! WORSHIP SERIES

Learning to Worship with All Your Heart: A Study in the Biblical Foundations of Worship

You are led into the rich teachings of worship in both the Old and the New Testaments. Learn the vocabulary of worship, be introduced to theological themes, and study various descriptions of worship. Each lesson inspires you to worship at a deeper level—from the inside out.

Rediscovering the Missing Jewel: A Study of Worship through the Centuries
This stretching course introduces you to the actual worship styles of Christians in other centuries and geographical locations. Study the history of the early, medieval, Reformation, modern, and contemporary periods of worship. Learn from them how your worship today may be enriched, inspired, and renewed. Each lesson introduces you to rich treasures of worship adaptable for contemporary use.

Renew Your Worship! A Study in the Blending of Traditional and Contemporary Worship
This inspiring course leads you into a deeper understanding and experience of your Sunday worship. How does worship bring the congregation into the presence of God, mold the people by the Word, and feed the believers spiritually? The answer to these and other questions will bring a new spiritual depth to your experience of worship.

Enter His Courts with Praise: A Study of the Role of Music and the Arts in Worship
This course introduces you to the powerful way the arts can communicate the mystery of God at work in worship. Music, visual arts, drama, dance, and mime are seen as means through which the gospel challenges the congregation and changes lives.

Rediscovering the Christian Feasts: A Study in the Services of the Christian Year
This stimulating and stretching course helps you experience the traditional church calendar with new eyes. It challenges the secular concept of time and shows how the practice of the Christian year offers an alternative to secularism and shapes the Christian's day-to-day experience of time, using the gospel as its grid.

Encountering the Healing Power of God: A Study in the Sacred Actions of Worship
This course makes a powerful plea for the recovery of those sacred actions that shape the spiritual life. Baptism, Communion, anointing with oil, and other sacred actions are all interpreted with reflection on the death and resurrection of Jesus. These actions shape the believer's spiritual experience into a continual pattern of death to sin and rising to life in the Spirit.

Empowered by the Holy Spirit: A Study in the Ministries of Worship
This course will challenge you to see the relationship between worship and life in the secular world. It empowers the believer in evangelism, spiritual formation, social action, care ministries, and other acts of love and charity.

Take all seven courses and earn a Certificate of Worship Studies (CWS). For more information, call the Institute for Worship Studies at (630) 510-8905.

INTRODUCTION

Empowered by the Holy Spirit: A Study in the Ministries of Worship may be used for personal study or a small-group course of study and spiritual formation. It is designed around thirteen easy-to-understand sessions. Each session has a two-part study guide. The first part is an individual study that each person completes privately. The second part is a one-hour interaction and application session that group members complete together (during the week or in an adult Sunday school setting). The first part helps you recall and reflect on what you've read, while the small-group study applies the material to each member's personal life and experience of public worship.

Empowered by the Holy Spirit is designed for use by one or more people. When the course is used in a group setting, the person who is designated as the leader simply needs to lead the group through the lesson step by step. It is always best to choose a leader before you begin.

Here are some suggestions for making your group discussions lively and insightful.

SUGGESTIONS FOR THE STUDENT

A few simple guidelines will help you use the study guide most effectively. They can be summarized under three headings: Prepare, Participate, and Apply.

Prepare

1. Answer each question in the study guide, "Part I: Personal Study," thoughtfully and critically.

2. Do all your work prayerfully. Prayer itself is worship. As you increase your knowledge of worship, do so in a spirit of prayerful openness before God.

Participate

1. Don't be afraid to ask questions. Your questions may give voice to the other members in the group. Your courage in speaking out will give others permission to talk and may encourage more stimulating discussion.

2. Don't hesitate to share your personal experiences. Abstract thinking has its place, but personal illustrations will help you and others remember the material more vividly.

3. Be open to others. Listen to the stories that other members tell, and respond to them in a way that does not invalidate their experiences.

Apply

1. Always ask yourself, "How can this apply to worship?"

2. Commit yourself to being a more intentional worshiper. Involve yourself in what is happening around you.

3. Determine your gifts. Ask yourself, "What can I do in worship that will minister to the body of Christ?" Then offer your gifts and talents to worship.

SUGGESTIONS FOR THE LEADER

Like the worship that it advocates, the group study in *Empowered by the Holy Spirit* is dialogic in nature. Because this study has been developed around the principles of discussion and sharing, a monologue or lecture approach will not work. The following guidelines will help you encourage discussion, facilitate learning, and implement the practice of worship. Use these guidelines with "Part II: Group Discussion" in each session.

1. Encourage the participants to prepare thoroughly and to bring their Bibles and study guides to each session.

2. Begin each session with prayer. Since worship is a kind of prayer, learning about worship should be a prayerful experience.

3. Discuss each question individually. Ask for several answers and encourage people to react to comments made by others.

4. Use a chalkboard or flip chart or dry-erase board. Draw charts and symbols that visually enhance the ideas being presented. Outline major concepts.

5. Look for practical applications of answers and suggestions that are offered. Try asking questions like, "How would you include this in our worship?" "How would you feel about that change?" "How does this insight help you to be a better worshiper?"

6. Invite concrete personal illustrations. Ask questions like, "Have you experienced that? Where? When? Describe how you felt in that particular situation."

7. When you have concluded Session 12, send the names and addresses of all the students who will complete the class to: Institute for Worship Studies, Box 894, Wheaton, IL 60189. We will then send a certificate of accomplishment for each student in time for you to distribute them during the last class. The cost of each certificate is $1.00. (Add $3.00 for postage and handling.)

One final suggestion: Purchase the larger work upon which this course is based, volume 7 of *The Complete Library of Christian Worship*. This volume, entitled *The Ministries of Christian Worship*, is a beautiful 8½-by-11-inch coffee table book that will inform your mind and inspire your heart through hours of reading and study.

PART I

THE

WORSHIPING

COMMUNITY

THE PUBLIC MINISTRY OF WORSHIP

A Study in the Ministries of Worship

When I was a child, my friends and I were always creating secret societies. We would band together, perhaps in a small treehouse that we had built, planning and concocting our own little "in-group." We created code words and a special language. We wanted to be known as a secret society. And we loved it when others heard about us and wanted to know our secrets or wanted to join us.

Secret societies and groups have always been a part of the religious landscape of the world. Many non-Christian religions are characterized by secrets known only to the in-group. In the period of the early church, there was a group known as the Gnostics that believed in a secret knowledge. The word *gnostic* means "knowledge." The Gnostics in the early church claimed to know saving information secretly handed down from the apostles.

The traditionalists within the early church fought the Gnostics "tooth and nail," insisting the Christian faith was a public faith known to all, not a secret religion known only to the few.

Christianity throughout the centuries has been a public faith, a faith whose content and practice is readily available to all who wish to know it or benefit by it. In this course of study, we want to understand the nature and content of worship's *public face* so we can enrich and empower the ministry of worship to those who are in the church.

THE BIBLICAL FOUNDATION

The New Testament records of the infant church clearly show that Christianity is not a secret society, but a group of people who wish to go public with their message and ministry.

In this infant community we can identify at least four ways in which the church exercised a public ministry.

The first of these is evangelism through preaching. Of course, the newly founded church did not have buildings, and it was not yet institutionalized. Consequently, preaching occurred in the streets and marketplaces of the villages and cities of the Roman world.

Immediately after Pentecost, the apostles went in response to the Great Commission (Acts 1:8) to spread the word to all that the end time had come, that the Messiah had appeared, and that people were to repent and turn to Christ for their salvation (see, for example, Acts 13).

A second way in which the church immediately exercised its public ministry was through the ministry of deliverance. The gospels record how Jesus delivered people from demonic possession and brought healing into their lives. This ministry of deliverance and healing did not end with Jesus, but continued through the apostolic ministry of the early church.

Early church records tell us that the apostles performed many signs and wonders among the people and that these miraculous happenings resulted not only in healings but also conversions and the growth of the church (Acts 5:12–16).

A third form of ministry in the early church was the production of literature that presented Christ (the gospels) and addressed problems that arose in the church (the epistles). Luke, for example, wrote two books, the Gospel of Luke and the Acts of the Apostles, to provide an accurate account of the life and work of Christ and the rise of the church (Luke 1:1–4). His work, along with the work of the other New Testament writers, became the authentic record of the Christian faith designed for reading and preaching in the early church.

A final public ministry of worship in the early church was its call to service. For example, Paul wrote, "I urge you, brothers, in view of God's mercy, to offer your bodies as living sacrifices, holy and pleasing to God—this is your spiritual act of worship" (Rom 12:1). This passage has always been interpreted to mean that worship is not only what we do when we gather but also what we do when we are scattered in the world, in our homes, at work or at leisure. Worship has to do, as the *Book of Common Prayer* so aptly states, "Not only with our lips, but also with our lives."

WORSHIP MINISTRIES TODAY

This theme, that worship has to do with all of life, has motivated the church throughout the centuries to develop ministries that proceed from the worshiping community to the world "out there."

In this course of study, we are going to look at these worship ministries. Let me outline that course of study for you now so that you will be able to start thinking about the broader ministry of worship.

First, the church of today is paying new attention to particular groups within the worshiping community that have not received adequate attention in the past—children, women, the disabled, and the culturally diverse.

Second, the church is now paying more attention to certain ministries that can and do occur within worship itself. These are the ministries of pastoral care, healing and deliverance, spiritual formation, and education.

Finally, new emphasis is being placed on the relationship between worship and the ministry of the church to the world. Areas of interest include hospitality, evangelism, and social justice.

CONCLUSION

This lesson has introduced us to the theme of worship and its related ministries. We want to be sensitized to the vision of a worship that moves us to action in this world. Even as God has acted in this world to bring healing and salvation, so we are called in worship to not only remember that action, but to continue God's action in the world by being God's agents of healing.

STUDY GUIDE

Read Session 1, "The Public Ministry of Worship,"
before starting the study guide.

PART I: PERSONAL STUDY

Complete the following questions individually.

1. *Life Connection*

◆ Did you ever belong to a "secret society" of your own making as a child? Tell about it._____

_____

_____

_____

_____

2. *Content Questions*

◆ Why is worship and the message it declares not a secret message, but a public message? _____

_____

_____

_____

◆ What are the four ways in which the Christian church made its views public?

   a. _____

   b. _____

   c. _____

   d. _____

◆ Read Acts 1:8, the Great Commission. What does it mandate?

_____

_____

_____

_____

◆ Read Acts 4:8–12. What was the content of Peter's sermon?

_____

_____

_____

_____

◆ Read Acts 5:12–16. What was the result of these miracles?

_____

_____

_____

_____

◆ Read Luke 1:1–4. How do you suppose the literature of the early church made the faith public? _____

_____

_____

_____

◆ Read Romans 12:1. How has the service to others rendered by Christians contributed to the growth of the church? _____

_____

_____

_____

◆ When we speak of the relationship between worship and the worshiping community, of whom are we speaking? _____

_____

_____

◆ When we speak of the relationship between worship and the ministries that occur in worship, to what ministries do we refer? _____

_____

_____

♦ When we speak of worship and its ministry to the world, what areas of concern do we address? _____

_____

_____

_____

_____

_____

3. *Application*

♦ How does worship minister to you? _____

_____

_____

_____

_____

PART II: GROUP DISCUSSION

The following questions are designed for group discussion. Share the insights you gained from your personal study in Part I.

Write out all answers that group members give to the questions on a chalkboard, a flipchart, or a dry erase board.

1. *Life Connection*

♦ Begin your discussion by asking group members to tell stories about secret societies they belonged to as children.

2. *Thought Questions*

♦ Why do you suppose the Christian faith is public, not secret?

♦ Review the four ways the Christian faith makes itself public.

♦ Read Acts 1:8. Was this mandate for the apostles only, or was it for all Christians everywhere? Explain.

- Read Acts 5:12–16. These kinds of miracles are reported to occur today, particularly in developing countries. Are there evidences of these kind of signs and wonders in your community? Should there be?
- Read Luke 1:1–4. Do most people today read the gospels as eyewitness accounts? How would you receive the Gospel of Luke if you had never heard of the Christian faith?
- Read Romans 12:1. How does our service in the world make public the faith we proclaim in worship?
- If we are to be concerned for worship ministry, who should we pay attention to within our own community? Why?
- If we are to be committed to ministry in our own worship, what kind of ministry will we address? Why?
- If we are committed to ministry to the world, what ministries will worship deal with? Why?

3. *Application*

- Evaluate how your church is doing in each of the four ways worship makes the message public (evangelism, signs and wonders, literature, service).
- Evaluate how your church is doing in its ministry to groups within the worshiping community and in its ministries that occur in worship, including ministry to the world.

LET THEM COME TO ME

A Study of Children in Worship

In our church we observe the ancient service called the great paschal vigil. This service is held on the night before Easter morning. In the early church the service lasted all night. But today in the modern church the service is usually about three hours in length, starting at 10:00 P.M. on Saturday and ending at 1:00 A.M. on Easter Sunday morning.

One significant aspect of the service is the Scripture reading. Scriptures are read that tell the story from the creation of the world to the restoration of the world. The present form of the service includes about ten passages. Between the readings the choir or the congregation, or both, sing appropriate hymns.

In this service families—mom, dad, and all the little ones—always sit together and listen to these readings. Recently a mother told me that in the middle of these long readings her daughter, age nine, looked up at her and said, "Mother, don't you just love these stories?"

I tell you this story because I think we underestimate how much children actually do enter into the worship of the church. In this study we will investigate the place of children in worship and will address ways to include them in worship.

JESUS AND CHILDREN

Mark records an instance in which people were bringing children to Jesus to be blessed by him. The disciples, thinking that this was a waste of Jesus' time, rebuked the parents and told them to go away. Jesus, the text says, was indignant. He then turned to his disciples and made two comments that define his attitude toward children.

First Jesus said, "Let the little children come to me, and do not hinder them, for the kingdom of God belongs to such as these." Then he said, "I tell you the truth, anyone who will not receive the kingdom of God like a little child will never enter it." Jesus then took the children in his arms and blessed them (Mark 10:13–16).

This beautiful picture of Jesus and the children speaks to us of the depth of a childlike trust, which is a gift. Unfortunately, many adults have exchanged the gift of childlike trust for a finely tuned intellectual understanding. According to Jesus the challenge of the adult is to achieve the trust of the child.

CHILDREN IN THE FOURFOLD PATTERN OF WORSHIP

The fourfold pattern of worship that has been presented in the Alleluia! Series on worship is the simple pattern of gathering, hearing God's word, celebrating at the table (or the alternative time of thanksgiving), and being dismissed. How do children relate to each part of worship?

The gathering is a joyous time, punctuated by a spirited procession and joyous singing. The children love this time of assembling for worship and in most churches are included.

Worship then shifts to the service of the word, which is dominated by Scripture readings and a sermon. Most children are restless during this part of worship. For this reason most churches that follow the fourfold pattern dismiss the children to a place where they have their own time of instruction. In many renewing churches the children's dismissal is accomplished this way: a junior high adolescent, carrying a banner, walks down the center aisle just before the service of the word begins, then turns and walks out of the sanctuary carrying the banner high. As he or she walks down the aisle, the children gather in a row and file out to their place of study in an orderly way.

As the worshiping community moves into Communion or the time of thanksgiving, the banner-bearer leads the children back into the sanctuary. They find their places with their parents and are present for Communion or the alternative time of thanksgiving.

Finally the community moves into the time of dismissal. Of course, the children are there as well.

CHILDREN'S SERMONS

Many churches have a time for children to come forward and hear a children's sermon before they are dismissed to their own place of instruction. Some people criticize these children's sermons because they are contrived and usually disrupt the flow of worship. So what should be done?

In renewing churches that follow the fourfold pattern, the children are brought by the banner-bearer to the front of the church, where they gather around the minister. The minister then tells them a Bible story (usually the gospel story of the day, drawn from the lectionary). Then the banner-bearer leads them to their place of study.

This scenario avoids a children's sermon that has no content, and it places the children's sermon in the worship in a way that avoids interrupting the flow of worship.

CHILDREN AND COMMUNION

The issue of children and Communion has been strongly debated within the church. And there are some very different opinions.

Some argue that children should not receive Communion until they understand what it is all about. Others argue that communion is a mystery that cannot be understood. It needs to be received with childlike faith and trust, and children may receive it.

Both camps at least agree that children should have the sense of being included. In those communities where children do not receive, they are still included. The child comes forward with his or her parents and crosses his or her hands across the chest. This is a signal that says, "I will not receive." But it also says, "Bless me." As the minister passes out the elements, the minister stops before the child, places a hand on the child's head and offers a blessing. In this way the child feels like a participant, not a spectator.

CONCLUSION

It is useful to compare the place of the children in the home to the place of the child in the worship family. How much, we might ask, is the child a participant in the home? And if the church is a family, how thoroughly should the child be integrated into the family life of the church?

Allow the words of Jesus, "Let the little children come to me," to be your guide as you think of the place of children in worship.

STUDY GUIDE

Read Session 2, "Let Them Come to Me,"
before starting the study guide.

PART I: PERSONAL STUDY

Complete the following questions individually.

1. *Life Connection*

◆ Do you have a story of a child entering into the worship of the church through his or her actions or a comment about worship made by a child that demonstrates understanding or interest in worship? Tell that story.

_____

_____

_____

_____

_____

2. *Content Questions*

◆ Read Mark 10:13–16. What does this text say about Jesus' attitude toward children? _____

_____

_____

_____

_____

◆ How do you interpret the phrase "let the little children come to me, and do not hinder them, for the kingdom of God belongs to such as these"?

_____

_____

_____

_____

_____

- How do you interpret the phrase "I tell you the truth, anyone who will not receive the kingdom of God like a little child will never enter it"?

  _____

  _____

  _____

  _____

- How may a child be involved in the fourfold pattern of worship?
  The gathering _____

  The word _____

  The eucharist (or alternative time of thanksgiving) _____

  _____

  The dismissal _____

  _____

- How may a church deal with the children's sermon? _____

  _____

  _____

  _____

- How may a church deal with children and Communion?

  _____

  _____

  _____

  _____

3. *Application*

- How would you personally like to see children involved in worship?

  _____

  _____

  _____

  _____

  _____

PART II: GROUP DISCUSSION

The following questions are designed for group discussion. Share the insights you gained from your personal study in Part I.

Write out all answers that group members give to the questions on a chalkboard, a flip chart, or a dry erase board.

1. *Life Connection*
   - Begin your discussion by asking the group to share stories about children in worship.

2. *Thought Questions*
   - Read Mark 10:13–16. Share ideas on how Jesus welcomed the little children.
   - Invite various people to interpret the phrase "let the little children come to me, and do not hinder them, for the kingdom of God belongs to such as these."
   - Invite people to interpret the phrase "I tell you the truth, anyone who will not receive the kingdom of God like a little child will never enter it."
   - Explore how children may be involved in each of the four parts of worship.
   - Explore options for the children's sermon.
   - Explore the issue of children receiving the eucharist.

3. *Application*
   - Evaluate the place of children in the worship of your church.
   - How can you improve the participation of children in worship?

SESSION 3

THE FEMALE SIDE OF THINGS
A Study of Women in Worship

The Bible and the history of the church include women of faith who have made an enormous impact on the church and in the world. I want to tell you about one of those women, a woman unknown to everybody except her family, her friends, and the people to whom she ministered—my mother.

My mother was born in 1902, was orphaned at age sixteen, was nurtured by the Spruce Street Baptist Church of Philadelphia, and graduated from Shelton College in New York City as the class valedictorian.

In 1927, at the age of twenty-five, she boarded a ship alone and sailed off to Africa as a missionary. A gifted linguist, she was given the special task of translating Scripture into one of many African languages. In addition, she (with my father, whom she met and married on the mission field) ministered in Mitulu, a settlement in the jungle in the heart of Belgian Congo (now Zaire) for many years.

That was, of course, decades ago—long before the women's movement of today. I remember, even as a child, thinking, "It's rather interesting that a woman like my mother can be sent by the church to the jungles of Africa to do ministry, yet here at home, it's only the men who serve as pastors." Of course, the place of women in worship has changed rather significantly in many churches today. And this raises the question of the study—the place of women in the church and its worship.

A BIBLICAL REFLECTION

We can begin our study of women in worship with two well-known examples from Scripture—Miriam and Huldah.

Miriam is well known because of the songs she sang to celebrate the victory of Yahweh over the Egyptians. Miriam took up the timbrel, a percussion instrument, and began to sing and dance. She chanted, "Sing to Yahweh, gloriously triumphant! Horse and rider are cast into the sea!" (a paraphrase of Exod 15:21). Years later

Micah associates Miriam's leadership in worship with a divine commissioning (Mic 6:3–5) acknowledging her calling to lead the community in worship.

A second famous woman involved in the worship of Israel was Huldah, a prophetess during the reign of Josiah, king of Judah. Josiah's ministers found a book in the temple that told of the covenant and how God's anger would be directed against Israel if they turned against him. The ministers were sent to Huldah to determine the significance of the book for Israel's worship. On the strength of her authority the book was regarded as authentic, and Israel was led into a revival of their relationship to Yahweh (see 2 Chron 34:14–33).

These two stories from the Old Testament seem to stand in sharp contrast to the seemingly stern attitude of Paul in 1 Corinthians 14:34–35. Here Paul admonishes women to "remain silent in the churches." At first look, Paul's statement seems to deny ordination to women. If understood in this strict way, this passage would also forbid women to teach classes or speak their mind about church life in congregational meetings as well.

However, some have argued that Paul's directive must have been meant for a special situation in the Corinthian church at that time and was not meant to be a universally established principle for all time. This argument seems to be substantiated by the presence of female leadership in the Philippian church, which Paul did not deny (see Phil 4:2–3), as well as female leadership in the Roman church, which Paul affirmed (Rom 16:1–2, 3, 6, 12, 15).

Other texts certainly imply an active female leadership role in the New Testament church. Today each denomination is facing these issues in a new way. Some allow women to become ordained to the work of ministry, others allow women to do everything in the church except the function of ministry prescribed for the ordained clergy. Even though no absolute and uniform practice has been established by all the churches, nearly all allow women to teach, read Scripture, sing, anoint with oil, and serve the bread and wine.

INCLUSIVE LANGUAGE

One matter that women have addressed in the last several decades is the use of exclusively male language. Many women have been sensitive to the overuse of male pronouns and to such words as *mankind, brotherhood,* and *the weaker sex.* This issue is most vexing in regard to traditional hymns characterized by male imagery.

Nancy Faus, in an article entitled "Issues in Developing Inclusive Language for Worship" in volume 7 of *The Complete Library of Christian Worship*, page 143, has provided us with some very sensible guidelines:

(1) If radical change is made in historical texts, an important sense of history is lost. Therefore, traditional hymns and prayers of the Christian church may need to remain in their original form.

(2) Memory of a personal association with hymns contributes to the richness and integrity of worship. Therefore, we are called to respect the memory banks of sisters and brothers, even when the words of that memory may bring uncomfortable images to other brothers and sisters or to us.

(3) New hymn texts and litanies need to express our world today and our part in modeling the equality of persons, whatever their race, culture, or sex. Therefore, we include in worship "texts which enlarge and deepen our faith through their poetic expression in late twentieth-century terms" ("Statement of Policy on Language for the Hymnal Project," of the Church of the Brethren, the General Conference Mennonite Church, and the Mennonite Church in North America, October 29, 1987).

(4) No one biblical translation is solely God's voice. The "original" Bible is one which does not exist in today's worship, for it was written in Hebrew, Aramaic, and Greek. Therefore, the use of Bible readings from an inclusive language lectionary help to increase our understandings of biblical truth and are often closer to the original intent and meaning of the Bible.

CONCLUSION

Not all churches are equally concerned over the women's issues in worship. The mainline Protestant churches, along with some voices in the Roman Catholic Church, seem to have the strongest influence in the matter. Leaders in most evangelical, fundamentalist, Pentecostal, and charismatic circles have not paid great attention to the matter. But in every church there are women who feel the issue and experience isolation because of it. Therefore, all churches should at least address the matter of women in worship and strive to be more inclusive. How far each church goes with the issue varies from denomination to denomination and local church to local church.

STUDY GUIDE

Read Session 3, "The Female Side of Things,"
before starting the study guide.

PART I: PERSONAL STUDY

The following questions are completed in individual study.

1. *Life Connection*
+ Recall a woman who made a significant impact on your personal life.

_____
_____
_____
_____
_____

+ Recall a woman in your church who made a significant impact on the church through a teaching or leadership ministry. _____

_____
_____
_____
_____

2. *Content Questions*
+ Read Exodus 15. How do you see the role of Miriam in this worship setting?

_____
_____
_____
_____

+ Read 2 Chronicles 34:14–33. What do you think the role of Huldah says about the place of women in the church and its worship? _____

_____
_____
_____
_____

- In light of these two Old Testament examples, how do you interpret the comment of Paul in 1 Corinthians 14:34–35? _____

  _____

  _____

  _____

  _____

- How do you understand the place of women in leadership in the following Scriptures?
  Philippians 4:2–3 _____

  _____

  _____

  Romans 16:1–2, 3, 6, 12, 15 _____

  _____

  _____

- Do you think Scripture is clearly against women's leadership, clearly for women's leadership, or ambiguous about women's leadership in the church and worship? Explain.
  clearly against _____

  _____

  clearly for _____

  _____

  ambiguous _____

  _____

- Use your own words to summarize the arguments of Nancy Faus regarding the use of inclusive language in worship.
  a. _____

  _____

  b. _____

  _____

  c. _____

  _____

  d. _____

  _____

3. *Application*

♦ What is your own opinion about women in the church and in worship leadership? What argument do you offer?

Opinion _____

_____

Argument _____

_____

PART II: GROUP DISCUSSION

The following questions are designed for group discussion. Share the insights you gained from your personal study in Part I.

Write out all answers that group members give to the questions on a chalkboard, a flip chart, or a dry erase board.

1. *Life Connection*

♦ Begin by asking members of the group to recall women who have influenced their lives.

♦ Continue by asking group members to recall a woman who made a significant impact on the church through her leadership ministry.

2. *Thought Questions*

♦ Review the role of Miriam in the worship of Israel recorded in Exodus 15. (There are contemporary versions of this song available. Sing it. Let the women lead it. Use percussion instruments and dance.)

♦ Read 2 Chronicles 34:14–33. How do you view Huldah's role in Israel?

♦ Read 1 Corinthians 14:34–35. Interpret this passage. What is Paul really saying?

♦ How do you interpret the following references to women in the church?

Philippians 4:2–3
Romans 16:1–2, 3, 6, 12, 15

- Review each of Nancy Faus's arguments for language in worship. How do you respond to each argument?

3. *Application*

- Evaluate the role of women in the worship of your church. What is the attitude of the church toward women in ministry? Women as worship leaders? Women as preachers? Women in teaching positions? Women as caregivers?

- Examine the language of your worship, hymns, preaching, and prayers. Are women included or excluded by the language? What is the level of interest in this matter in your church? What changes, if any, should be made?

SPECIAL PEOPLE

A Study of the Worship of People with Disabilities

 One of the most well-known disabled people in the world is Joni Erickson Tada.

Most people know something of her story. At age eighteen, full of life and looking forward to her future, she dove into a pool, broke her neck, and became paralyzed from the neck down.

In spite of her paralysis, Joni is an accomplished painter, the writer of several best-selling books, and a speaker at Christian events all over the world. In a recent speech at Wheaton College, where I teach, she told the student body, "I'm looking forward to the resurrection! When I get my new body, I'm going to ask Jesus for the first dance." Her story is one of courage and success. But there is still the pain and suffering that all people with disabilities experience. How should the church respond to those who are challenged by a disabling condition? That is the question of this study.

A BIBLICAL PERSPECTIVE

A quick reading of the gospels shows that Jesus has a special place in his heart for the poor, the sick, and the disabled.

One of the most interesting stories concerning a disabled person is the account of a crippled women healed on the Sabbath. This woman, the text tells us, had been suffering for eighteen years. Jesus healed her instantly, and "she straightened up and praised God" (worship is the appropriate response to God's healing).

The synagogue rulers, however, were not impressed. Jesus had healed on the Sabbath, and there was a rule against working on the Sabbath. When they came after Jesus, he replied, "You hypocrites! Doesn't each of you on the Sabbath untie his ox or donkey from the stall and lead it out to give it water? Then should not this woman, a daughter of Abraham, . . . be set free on the Sabbath day from what bound her?"

Jesus' pointed question elicited an interesting and telling response. "All his opponents were humiliated, but the people were delighted with all the wonderful things he was doing" (Luke 13:10–17).

In this text we see not only Jesus' deep compassion for the hurting but also his care and loving concern for those who suffer disabling conditions.

Perhaps Jesus' view of the disabled was expressed when he said, "I tell you the truth, whatever you did for one of the least of these brothers of mine, you did for me" (Matt 25:40). We are called to live out Jesus' attitude in the local church.

THE DISABLED IN WORSHIP

Worship is the assembly of *all* of God's people—all conditions, all colors, and all sorts. So it is obvious that the worship of the church should include the disabled.

But how? Howard Rice, a wheelchair worshiper, has written an article entitled "Planning for Disabled People" (in *The Library of Christian Worship*, vol. 7, pp. 154–59). We will draw on his suggestions.

First, worship planners must be concerned for space. The space in which we worship must be conducive for all to worship. Worship not only includes mobility, it also involves the ability to hear and see. Rice suggests that the planners of worship take the following ten questions into serious consideration:

- How could a person in a wheelchair enter our building?
- Is there a place for a wheelchair within the congregation?
- Are the restroom doors and stalls wide enough to admit a wheelchair?
- Do we have materials in Braille for use by those with severe visual impairments?
- Do we have large-print hymnals?
- Do we use the services of a signer for the benefit and inclusion of persons with hearing difficulties?
- Does our church have handrails on all stairs?
- How safe are the floors for people on crutches?
- Do we have drivers who will pick up people unable to drive?
- Is there at least one washbasin no more than thirty inches high in the men's and women's restrooms?

Once a church has addressed the matter of space, it must look at the role of the usher, the language of worship itself, and the leaders of worship.

The usher needs to be trained how to greet and help the impaired.

The language of worship needs to include the disabled and avoid stereotypical language, such as blind, deaf, or lame.

The kind of people who lead worship sends a direct message to the disabled. So include the disabled in areas of worship, such as the reading of Scripture, singing, ushering, and greeting.

CONCLUSION

We are living in a rapidly changing world where the disabled are finding a new place. Nevertheless, according to Howard Rice, the two places in the world that are least accessible to the disabled are medical clinics and churches.

If we truly believe God's church is one people, then we, as the people of God, need to ask how can we make our place of worship more hospitable for those who are disabled.

And once we have answers for the questions, we must act on them!

STUDY GUIDE

*Read Session 4, "Special People,"
before starting the study guide.*

PART I: PERSONAL STUDY

Complete the following questions individually.

1. *Life Connection*

◆ Recall the personal experience of someone who is disabled. Comment on how that person has found life more difficult because of his or her disability.

_____

_____

_____

_____

_____

2. *Content Questions*

◆ Read Luke 13:10–17. Imagine you are going to turn this story into a drama to be told in worship. How would you do it? Develop the story in the space below, using staging, actors, and dialogue. _____

_____

_____

_____

_____

_____

◆ Read Matthew 25:40. This passage reveals the heart of Jesus toward the less fortunate. What words would you use to describe Jesus' attitude toward those who are physically or mentally challenged? _____

_____

_____

_____

◆ Use your own words to paraphrase the ten questions Howard Rice suggests for the church to consider to be sensitive to the disabled.

_____

_____

_____

_____

_____

_____

_____

_____

_____

_____

◆ Explain how the following can be sensitive to the needs of the disabled.
The usher _____

_____

_____

The language of worship _____

_____

_____

The worship leaders _____

_____

_____

3. *Application*
◆ What can you do to help the disabled feel more welcome?

_____

_____

_____

_____

PART II: GROUP DISCUSSION

The following questions are designed for group discussion. Share the insights you gained from your personal study in Part I.

Write out all answers that group members give to the questions on a chalkboard, a flip chart, or a dry erase board.

1. *Life Connection*

◆ Begin your discussion by asking members of the group to share stories of friends who are disabled. How has the church met or not met their needs?

2. *Thought Questions*

◆ Read Luke 13:10–17. Have people share the dramatic presentation they created from this passage. Take the time to actually do someone's dramatic presentation of the passage.

◆ Read Matthew 25:40. What does this passage have to say about Jesus' heart toward the physically and mentally challenged?

3. *Application*

◆ Spend a good deal of time discussing the ten suggestions made by Howard Rice. Analyze your church in terms of these ten questions. Put the ten questions in a column on the left side of the board. Create another column entitled "This Church" on the right side of the board. Now answer each question.

◆ Create a third column on the board and label it "What Can We Do?" Brainstorm how your church can become more sensitive to the needs of the disabled.

◆ Wrap up your session by addressing how the ushers, the language of worship, and the worship leaders may become more helpful to the physically and mentally challenged. Ask, "How can the disabled be included as worship leaders, ushers, greeters?"

MANY FACES

A Study in the Cultural Diversity of Worship

 One of the courses I teach in the graduate school of Wheaton College is called "Historical Theology."

Wheaton graduate school includes an international community of students. Nevertheless, it was a surprise several years ago to discover that among the twenty-two students in my historical theology course, thirteen nationalities were represented. That was the broadest diversity of students I have ever had in that course. Needless to say, we were all enriched by each other's backgrounds and the theological insights that each culture brought.

In most churches, worship is marked by homogeneity. Our church may be African-American, Asian, Spanish, or Caucasian. But seldom, except in the inner city, do we find churches characterized by strong ethnic diversity. Those who study the changing cultural shape of American society tell us that a cultural shift is in the making and that churches need to be prepared to accept cultural diversity. In this study we want to face the phenomenon of cultural diversity in worship and ask how we can get ready to worship in a multicultural setting.

THE BIBLICAL BACKGROUND

We are all aware that the Old Testament records God's saving action with the Hebrew people. Israel's faith in Yahweh was a national faith. God was their God. Israel was God's people.

One of the most revolutionary announcements of the Christian faith, which had its roots in Jewish thought, was that God in Christ was for all the peoples of the earth.

This truth is first encountered in the story of the three wise men who came from afar (other countries and nationalities) to worship Jesus (see Matt 2:1–12). It is next encountered in the vision given to Peter when he was told to go to the house of Cornelius, a Gentile. The upshot of the story is that Cornelius became a Christian and was baptized. The other disciples later challenged the baptism of Cornelius and the inclusion of the Gentiles in the church. When Peter explained the vision from God, they all concluded, "So then, God has granted even the Gentiles repentance unto life" (Acts 10:1–11:18).

Later, Paul, reflecting on the Body of Christ, exclaimed: "we were all baptized by one Spirit into one body—whether Jews or Greeks, slave or free—and we were all given the one Spirit to drink" (1 Cor 12:13).

A quick review of the history of the church shows that the Christian church has been established among all the nationalities of the world. Christianity is a religion of all classes, all colors, and all the peoples of the world.

THE CHANGING PATTERN OF CULTURE IN AMERICA

Unfortunately, most of the churches of the world are divided according to class and color. The American church is no exception. We have churches dominated by the rich, churches dominated by the poor, churches dominated by whites, blacks, Asians, Hispanics, Polish, and innumerable other groups.

The nonwhite population is growing, and integrated neighborhoods are becoming places of cultural diversity. Sociologist Zondra Lindblade reports that demographers project the white and non-Hispanic population to decline from its present 83 percent to 65 percent of the population by the year 2010. The 12 percent of the population that is African-American will remain steady; Asian and other groups will increase to 5 percent of the population. And the Hispanic population will double in size to 18 percent of the total population.

The trend toward a more culturally diverse society can already be seen in the population shift recorded in a recent study. ("The Emergence of a Mulitcultural Society," in volume 7 of *The Complete Library of Christian Worship*, pages 191–93.)

Metro area	Percent minority in 1990	Change in percent minority since 1980
San Antonio	55.7	+ 2.8
Miami	52.2	+13.2
Los Angeles	50.2	+11.1
Houston	42.1	+ 7.3
San Diego	34.6	+ 8.5
Dallas/Ft. Worth	30.3	+ 6.1

WORSHIP SENSITIVE TO CULTURAL DIVERSITY

Is there such a thing as culturally sensitive worship? First of all, let it be said that the content of worship is not subject to change. Christian worship has always remembered, proclaimed, and enacted God's saving deeds culminating in Jesus Christ. In addition, the shape of worship does not need to change. All worship gathers the people, proclaims the word, celebrates at the table, gives thanks, and goes forth to serve. These are the constants of worship regardless of national or cultural diversity. So what must change?

First, and most importantly, what must change is the attitude of the people. We must all affirm with Paul that "there is neither Jew nor Greek, slave nor free, male nor female, for you are all one in Christ Jesus" (Gal 3:28).

Second, when our attitudes have changed to a more inclusive acceptance of the entire body of Christ, then the style of our worship will become more inclusive. Style is primarily associated with music and ceremony. Our music will broaden to include the songs of other cultures. Our ceremony will draw from other cultures and reflect traditions other than our own.

CONCLUSION

The world, everyone is saying, is changing. For example, when I think of the changes that have occurred since my father was born in 1900, my head spins. These changes—cultural changes, technical changes, communication changes, and population shifts—are forcing the church to change, too. Are you ready?

STUDY GUIDE

Read Session 5, "Many Faces,"
before starting the study guide.

PART I: PERSONAL STUDY

Complete the following questions individually.

1. *Life Connection*

◆ Recall the most international and intercultural event you ever attended. What was your experience? _____

_____

_____

_____

_____

2. *Content Questions*

◆ If you were a Jew of the first century who had it drilled into you that God was the God of one people—Israel—how would you have responded to the Christian proclamation that God was the God of *all* peoples, not just Israel? _____

_____

_____

_____

◆ Read Matthew 2:1–12. How does this passage demonstrate that the Christian faith is to be extended beyond the borders of Israel?

_____

_____

_____

_____

_____

- Read Acts 10:1–11:18. Have you ever given much thought to the struggle it must have been for those early Christian Jews to recognize that God's love for humanity went beyond Israel to all the peoples of the world? Have you yourself ever grasped the international and intercultural mixture of the Christian faith? _____

_____

_____

_____

_____

- Make a graph showing the change that is taking place in the cultural makeup of America.

- What aspects of worship remain the same in the face of cultural diversity?

_____

_____

_____

_____

_____

- Explain how the *style* of worship will change as our churches become more culturally diverse. _____

_____

_____

_____

_____

3. *Application*

♦ Summarize your own attitude toward a culturally diverse congregation and worship. _____

_____

_____

_____

PART II: GROUP DISCUSSION

The following questions are designed for group discussion. Share the insights you gained from your personal study in Part I.

Write out all answers that group members give to the questions on a chalkboard, a flip chart, or a dry erase board.

1. *Life Connection*

♦ Begin your discussion by asking people to recall the most international or intercultural event ever attended.

2. *Thought Questions*

♦ Ask people to put themselves into the position of a Jew in the first century. How would they have responded to the message that God is love for all the peoples of the world?

♦ Interpret Matthew 2:1–12. How does this passage demonstrate the international and intercultural nature of the Christian faith?

♦ Read Acts 10:1–11:18 (or tell the story). How does this story speak to our prejudices?

♦ Has the cultural change that is taking place in America reached your city or town? Identify evidences of this change.

♦ Explain why the *content* and *structure* of worship will remain the same regardless of cultural change.

♦ Explain why the *style* of worship will undergo change as the cultural makeup of the people changes.

3. *Application*

◆ Evaluate the present state of your church. Is it ready for cultural change? What must it do to meet the needs of a culturally changing neighborhood?

◆ How should the *style* of your worship change to meet the changing culture?

◆ Take some time to sing the songs of other cultures. (Most new hymnbooks include a good selection of songs and hymnody from a variety of cultures.)

PART II

MINISTRY

WITHIN THE

WORSHIPING

COMMUNITY

COME UNTO ME

A Study in Worship and Pastoral Care

Some time ago a good friend of mine went through a very bitter divorce. It was one of these situations where the spouse had been unfaithful. And what made matters even more difficult was the fact that the divorcing couple had several small children.

When the divorce proceedings were over, my friend felt emotionally dissipated and spiritually flat. Her hopes had been dashed, her life totally disrupted, her family left in shambles. And then she began to doubt God. In a letter she wrote, "Bob, I can barely go to church and I can't receive the bread and wine."

I wrote back to her immediately and said, "Now, more than ever, you need to be in worship; now more than ever stretch forth your hand and receive the bread. Bite down hard on the bread and claim everything that God has done for you in Jesus Christ. Drink of the cup and let the wine run through your whole body because that is Jesus who is there to touch you, heal you, and make you whole!"

Pastoral care has to do with the healing that comes our way through worship. In this study we want to examine how that happens.

THE BIBLICAL BACKGROUND

The Scriptures have a great deal to say about illness and wellness. Illness, of course, can be defined as emotional sickness, physical illness, or even a disorder of the mind. Jesus repeatedly brought healing to the sick (Matt 9:1–8, 27–34). Jesus saw illness as a contradiction to God's plan for the creation. In bringing healing to those people Jesus foreshadowed the new heavens and the new earth, where sin, sickness, and sorrow will be no more (Rev 21:1–4). The apostles continued the ministry of healing in Jesus' name (Acts 5:12, 15–16).

Sickness in the Christian vision of reality is seen against the backdrop of the Christian worldview. This worldview can be succinctly summarized in the biblical narrative, which says: God created a perfect world; the power of the evil one (Satan) has distorted God's good creation resulting in all kinds of dislocation, including sickness, violence, etc.; God became incarnate in Jesus, the Messiah and Savior of the world; by his death and resurrection Jesus Christ has dethroned the powers of the evil one; when Christ returns and judgment day occurs all evil will be eradicated; in that day the new heavens and the new earth will appear as a restored paradise. While this biblical narrative is much more complex than our brief outline, it is the context in which Christians are called to think about illness.

PASTORAL CARE AND WORSHIP

How does this worldview and the hope for the cure of all emotional, physical, and mental disorders relate to worship?

In worship we proclaim and enact the Christian worldview. And when we do our worship with faith and intention, God ministers to us through the gathering, the service of the word, the eucharist, and the dismissal.

I am convinced that hurting people find more in worship than those whose lives are running smoothly. Think, for example, of those times when you have been sick in mind, body, or spirit. When you went to worship, were you more attentive? Did you listen for a word from God? Did you receive the bread and wine with a prayer for your healing? Did you hope that the benediction, the blessing from God, would fall on your life? In weakness we seem to be more open and more vulnerable to God than we are when we are strong and full of life.

HEALING WORDS AND ACTIONS OF WORSHIP

Let's look at some of the words and actions of worship that may bring healing into our lives.

In many churches, the gathering includes a brief time for the confession of sins. Consider the power of the following confession to bring release from the sickness of guilt, flooding the penitent with cleansing from God:

Most Merciful God
We confess that we have sinned against you
in thought, word, and deed
by what we have done,
and by what we have left undone.
We have not loved you with our whole heart;

We have not loved our neighbours as ourselves;
We are truly sorry and we humbly repent.
For the sake of your Son, Jesus Christ,
have mercy on us and forgive us;
that we may delight in your will,
and walk in your ways,
to the glory of your Name. Amen. (from the *Book of Common Prayer*)

In the service of the word, the readings of Scripture may speak to your situation in a special way. This may not always be the case in the narrative literature, but the psalms or the gospel may often relate to you in a way that you yourself receive it. Then, of course, there is the sermon. The pastor may reflect on the passage and use an illustration or a phrase in such a way that it speaks healingly to your situation.

At bread and wine, the saving and healing action of God that brings healing to the whole world is being enacted. To receive pastoral care at bread and wine, receive with intention. You can say, "O Lord, you who are the healer of the universe, heal my condition now as I receive the food of your redeeming and healing power."

Furthermore the songs that are song at bread and wine can also minister healing. If the congregation sings "When I Survey the Wondrous Cross" or "Jesus, Remember Me" or other moving Communion songs, the power of the words and the sound can bring healing into your situation.

Then there is the benediction. In these words God blesses you. Examine the words, for example, of what is called the Aaronic blessing and sense the healing that is brought to life in these words:

The Lord bless you
and keep you;
The Lord make his face shine upon you
and be gracious to you;
The Lord turn his face toward you
and give you peace. (Num 6:24–26)

WORSHIP RITUALS FOR SPECIAL SITUATIONS

Finally, a word needs to be said about special situations in which a ritual focuses intentionally on the matter of wellness.

The ritual of anointing with oil for healing (see Jas 5:14–16) has made a significant comeback as an act of worship.

The anointing with oil with the laying on of hands and a prayer for healing may occur in a regular service of worship (usually during the eucharist) or may be a special service in the hospital or any private place.

The illness may be named. Then the ill person may be anointed with oil in the sign of the cross, in the name of the Father, the Son, and the Holy Spirit. The following prayer or something like it may be said:

> May the Holy Spirit bring healing into your life—
> mind, body, and soul.
> [Here words may be said pertaining to the special circumstance]
> And may you be filled with the presence of Jesus.

CONCLUSION

There is a saying, "Don't go to worship for what you can get, go to worship for what you can give," that is a half-truth. We do give God worship. But in worship God gives to us. God brings to us the benefit of the healing that God accomplished for us in Jesus Christ.

The next time you go to worship, be open to the healing God can bring to your life.

STUDY GUIDE

*Read Session 6, "Come unto Me,"
before starting the study guide.*

PART I: PERSONAL STUDY

Complete the following questions individually.

1. *Life Connection*
* Give an example of pastoral care and healing you or a friend of yours received through the church and its worship. _____

_____

_____

_____

_____

2. *Content Questions*
* Read Matthew 9:1–8, 27–34. Turn one of these two stories into a drama. Decide the setting, the actors, and the dialogue. Sketch it out below.

_____

_____

_____

_____

_____

_____

_____

* How is sickness of any kind interpreted against the backdrop of the Christian worldview? _____

_____

_____

_____

_____

• Why should worship be a setting for healing and wholeness?

_____

_____

_____

_____

_____

• How may a confession of sin in worship bring healing and wholeness?

_____

_____

_____

_____

• How may the service of the word speak a word of healing and wholeness into a person's life? _____

_____

_____

_____

_____

• How may healing and wholeness be experienced in the eucharist?

_____

_____

_____

_____

• How may healing and wholeness be experienced in the dismissal?

_____

_____

_____

_____

• How may the anointing with oil and the laying on of hands result in healing and wholeness? _____

_____

_____

_____

_____

3. *Application*

◆ Do you personally have an area in your life that needs healing and wholeness? What is it? _____

_____

_____

_____

_____

PART II: GROUP DISCUSSION

The following questions are designed for group discussion. Share the insights
you gained from your personal study in Part I.

Write out all answers that group members give to the questions on a
chalkboard, a flip chart, or a dry erase board.

1. *Life Connection*

◆ Begin by asking various members of the group to give examples from
their own lives or from the life of a friend who has received healing and
pastoral care from worship.

2. *Thought Questions*

◆ Have the stories of Matthew 9:1–8 and 27–34 presented. Act them out,
and then discuss their message concerning healing and wholeness.

◆ Interpret sickness against the backdrop of the Christian worldview.

◆ Find out why people think worship should be a setting for healing and
wholeness.

◆ How may a confession of sin bring healing and wholeness? Give an example.

◆ How may preaching bring healing and wholeness? Give an example.

◆ How may Communion bring healing and wholeness? Give an example.

◆ How may the dismissal bring healing and wholeness? Give an example.

- How may the prayer for healing, with the anointing of oil, bring healing and wholeness?

3. *Application*
- Evaluate the worship of your church and its effectiveness as a place of healing. If it isn't, why isn't it? If it is, why is it?
- Plan a worship service in which healing and wholeness are made more intensely available.
- Consider having a weekly or monthly service of healing. What would this service look like? How would the people respond?

IN THE NAME OF JESUS

A Study in Worship and Deliverance

Back in the early 1970s I had a very unusual experience, one that has never been repeated. Late one night I received a call from a frantic mother who said, "My daughter is in trouble, can you come quickly?" I immediately went to find Kathy in a catatonic state. But she was coherent enough to say, "Go to Bill, he needs you more." Bill was in another room lying on a couch. His eyes were glazed over. His mouth was wide open. And he was motionless. I called to him, but there was no answer.

Apprehending that I could be dealing with something mysterious and demonic, I leaned over Bill's face and said, "Who are you?" A voice came from Bill's still mouth saying, "I am legion." I knew that *legion* meant "many," and I knew I was up against a power over which I had no control. I had never done this before, but I placed my hands around Bill's head and said, "In the name of Jesus and by the power of his blood, I command you to return to hell." After a long night of wrestling with this power in the name of Jesus, a deliverance did occur. I saw a movement pass through Bill's entire body, beginning at the bottom of his feet. As his body heaved and fell off the couch, an invisible force left Bill. He was delivered.

I have never had such an experience again. Despite the histrionic excess of some television preachers, I do think that there is a reality to the demonic and that we can deal with it in worship and special acts of deliverance.

THE BIBLICAL BACKGROUND

The biblical background for deliverance is very much the same as the biblical background for illness: God created a perfect world; this world has fallen away from God due to powers that have sought to destroy God's good creation; God has come in Jesus Christ to destroy the powers and to deliver and rescue the creation and establish a new heaven and a new earth. (In the Old Testament the Exodus event is a deliverance and a liberation that stands as a type of God's ultimate deliverance of the world from evil.)

In the New Testament era we see this theology in action in the ministry of Jesus. He delivers those who are oppressed by demonic forces (for example, Mark 5:1–20). The healing of the demon-possessed man illustrates the entire narrative of a dislocated world delivered and relocated in God.

THE DIFFERENCE BETWEEN DELIVERANCE AND HEALING

It is very important to make a distinction between healing and deliverance. Healing has to do with a sickness of mind, body, or emotion. Sicknesses result from accidents, broken relations, germs, and so forth. These sicknesses are not a result of demonic activity. (Some Christians argue that all sickness is caused by demonic power. For example, they speak of the need to be delivered from the demon of the cold or the flu or other illnesses.) Sickness demands healing, but situations that require deliverance are special and more occasional.

According to Francis McNutt, a Roman Catholic in the ministry of deliverance, there are three tests to determine if a deliverance rather than a healing is needed:

- Is there a history of compulsive behavior (common compulsions include drug addiction, alcoholism, attempted suicides, and overeating)?
- Does the person coming for prayer feel the problem is demonic in origin?
- Has the prayer for inner healing been ineffective?

THE PRAYER FOR DELIVERANCE

While the prayer for deliverance is an act of worship, it is not usually done in the normal service of worship. Generally it is done with a small group of concerned people in an act of worship separated from the Sunday communal act.

The prayer differs from the prayer of healing in that it is directed toward the demonic in the name of Christ and is a command, not a petition.

The following procedure for a prayer of deliverance is drawn from the pattern suggested by Francis McNutt in his article, "Deliverance and Exorcism," in volume 7 of *The Complete Library of Christian Worship.*

- Pray for protection. There is an instance in the New Testament where a demonic power was set loose, only to beat and overpower the community gathered to deliver the demon-possessed person (see Acts 19:15–16). For this reason it is always important to pray for protection that no evil force will harm anyone in the room.

- Bind the enemy. Pray next that the enemy may be bound by the power of Christ and lose any power to resist. Even as Jesus bound the powers of evil (see Matt 12:22–30, especially v. 29), so we can bind the demonic, but in his name only.
- Identify the oppression. A demon is usually identified by its primary activity (the spirit of self-destruction, the spirit of fear, the spirit of depression, etc.). This identification may occur in one of three ways:

> The person asking for prayer may already be able to name the power.
> The person praying may have the power of discernment.
> The demon may offer its name when commanded to identify itself.

- Casting out the demon. First ask the person tormented by the demonic power to cast out the demon. If this fails, then the minister of prayer should command the demon to leave. It is important that the command be "in the name of Jesus." We do not ourselves have the power of deliverance, which is God's prerogative only.
- After the deliverance. Once a person has been delivered, four steps should be taken:
  1. The minister should pray for God to fill the person's life with the presence of Jesus.
  2. The person should be taught to break the pattern of sin that led to the problem.
  3. The person should be instructed to adopt a spiritual discipline of prayer and Scripture reading.
  4. The person should become an active member of a Christian church.

CONCLUSION

For some people this will have been a hard session. Most of us do not see or experience this kind of demonic activity, so it may feel remote or strange.

History, however, attests to its reality. The church has always recognized the power of the demonic and has used rituals similar to those described above to deal with demonic possession.

Today this kind of ministry is especially relevant to those who have been overtaken by drug addiction, as well as to persons living in more primitive societies, where the activity of the demonic is quite apparent.

STUDY GUIDE

Read Session 7, "In the Name of Jesus,"
before starting the study guide.

PART I: PERSONAL STUDY

Complete the following questions individually.

1. *Life Connection*
- Recall an experience from your own life or from someone you know of deliverance from a demonic oppression. _____

_____
_____
_____
_____

2. *Content Questions*
- What is the biblical background for any ministry of deliverance?

_____
_____
_____
_____
_____

- How does the exodus event illustrate the basic theme of deliverance?

_____
_____
_____
_____
_____

- How does Jesus express the ministry of deliverance? _____

_____
_____
_____
_____

◆ Read Mark 5:1–20. Turn this story into a drama with a setting, actors, and dialogue. _____

_____

_____

_____

_____

_____

_____

_____

◆ What is the difference between deliverance and healing?
Healing is _____

_____

_____

Deliverance is _____

_____

_____

_____

◆ What are the three tests that determine if a deliverance, not a healing, is necessary?
a. _____

_____

b. _____

_____

c. _____

_____

◆ Use your own words to summarize the procedure for deliverance.
a. _____

_____

b. _____

_____

c. _____

_____

- What should be done for a person who has been delivered?
  a. _____
  b. _____
  c. _____
  d. _____

3. *Application*

- Is there anything in your life from which you feel a need for deliverance?

  _____
  _____
  _____
  _____

PART II: GROUP DISCUSSION

The following questions are designed for group discussion. Share the insights you gained from your personal study in Part I.

Write out all answers that group members give to the questions on a chalkboard, a flip chart, or a dry erase board.

1. *Life Connection*

- Begin by asking various members of the class to talk about their own or somebody else's experience with deliverance.

2. *Thought Questions*

- Does the biblical story encourage a ministry of deliverance? How?
- Does the exodus event illustrate a deliverance situation? How?
- Perform the drama of Mark 5:1–20. How does this story illustrate Jesus' approach to deliverance?
- Compare a healing to a deliverance.
- What are the three tests to determine that a deliverance is needed, not a healing?

- What is the procedure for doing a deliverance?
- What should be done for a person who has been delivered?

3. *Application*
- Evaluate the ministry of deliverance at your church. If you do not have one, should you? If you do have one, is it appropriate or is it excessive?
- What steps would you take to improve your ministry of deliverance?

GROW IN CHRIST

A Study in Worship and Spiritual Formation

I have always been fond of one-liners. I admire people who can
think them up or quip them extemporaneously. I'm not good at
coming up with one-liners, so I pick them up from other people.

I want to share a one-liner with you that I think captures the essence of spiritual
formation in worship.

I don't even know the name of the person who gave me this one-liner, but I
remember he was a professor of ethics at the University of Chicago. We had a chance
encounter in Michigan, where we were both vacationing. As we were talking about
the faith and the place of worship in our lives, he said, "Bob, I want nothing more
than that the word of God take up residence in my life and shape me into
Christ-likeness."

"That's it! That's it!" I thought to myself. "That's the spiritual goal of worship.
That's what everyone should want—the word to take up residence within and shape
us into Christ-likeness."

In this session we want to understand how worship can accomplish spiritual
formation in our life.

THE BIBLICAL AND THEOLOGICAL BASIS

We have already covered the biblical and theological base of worship. These
principles remain the same for spiritual formation, so I will simply summarize them here:

- Worship celebrates the mighty deeds of God's salvation. Christian worship
  remembers, proclaims, and enacts the living, the dying, and the rising of
  Christ and the overthrow of the powers of evil.
- Through the proclamation of the word (preaching) and enactment of the
  Christ event (eucharist) the saving, healing, and forming power of God is
  made available to the worshiping community.

With these two basic principles in mind, let's ask how worship actually forms our spiritual life so that the word of God resides within us and shapes us into Christ-likeness.

How Worship Forms Us Spiritually

Spiritual formation in worship occurs in two ways. First, worship is a rehearsal of our relationship with God. What forms, shapes, and molds our person, our values, our character, our integrity is the frequent encounter with the living Christ in the liturgy. What God is about in history is the formation of the body of Christ, the people within a people, the society within a society, the fellowship in faith. This family is stamped by a character—the character of Christ, delivered by the Spirit, especially in worship. From a human standpoint, this means that spiritual formation occurs not merely from being *at* worship, but from allowing the vision rehearsed in worship—the vision that sweeps from re-creation to creation—to become the vision out of which and by which each worshiper lives.

Second, worship through the Christian year shapes our lives after the pattern of Jesus. The power of the church year is that it provides an external organization of time through which an internal experience of the Christian vision of reality is experienced. It serves as an elongated service of worship that stretches across the year. In Advent, the church enters the Old Testament experience of longing for the coming of the Messiah and the promise of a restored earth where swords will be turned into plowshares. At Christmas, the people of God reflect with awe and wonder on the Incarnate One—God with us. At Epiphany, the church witnesses the manifestation of Christ to the whole world. During Lent, Christians travel the road of death through Holy Week into death itself. They let their sins be nailed to the cross and buried in the tomb. On Easter, Christians experience the resurrection as a living reality. Finally, Pentecost becomes the experience of the Spirit, the outward mission of the church toward the world.

These examples describe how corporate spiritual formation becomes the impetus for daily spiritual formation. Every day has its meaning rooted in the event that broke the powers of death, shifted history into the end times, and shaped God's people toward the end of history—the new heavens and the new earth.

Four Ways to Bring Worship and Spirituality Together

As we think about our worship and our spirituality, we need to ask ourselves what steps we need to take to bring worship and spirituality together. We want to grow, and we want the people of the church to grow as well. Here are four suggestions.

First, restore a Christocentric focus to worship. The whole theme of heavenly worship envisioned in Revelation 4–5 centers on Christ. Christ is worthy to receive glory and honor and power because he "created all things" (Rev 4:11). He is worthy because he was slain and has redeemed us to God by his blood (see Rev 5:9). Christian spirituality is rooted in this vision of life and must therefore grow out of it. It is not mere do-goodism or a head belief, but a life lived in the conviction that the Christ of the Bible is the meaning-giver, that all things, including one's whole life, is of him, through him, and to him.

Second, restore an order for worship that tells and acts out the fundamental story of human existence. Churches need to find an external order in worship that tells and acts out the story so that our internal experience of being encountered by the story will be maximized. The rule of thumb for order in worship is rooted in the nature of worship. If worship tells and acts out the story, then the order must be the servant of the message. The ancient order of worship was a single fourfold action:

- Preparation to worship
- Encounter with God through the word together with response
- Encounter with God through eucharist together with response
- Dismissal

This order organizes the internal experience of:

- Coming before God
- Listening to God speak and responding to this spoken word
- Receiving Christ through the symbols of bread and wine
- Dismissal to live in Christ's name

The worshiper who comes to worship with an intelligent understanding of worship and with intentionality is carried through an actual rehearsal of her or his relationship to God through the order for worship that organizes the relationship. Worship is then the context in which a meaningful encounter with God actually takes place. In the preparation, forgiveness of sins known and unknown is made; in the word, God addresses the worshiper with the saving message; in the eucharist, Christ encounters the worshiper in a healing way. While this relationship may happen on a subliminal level without understanding or intention, the probability of its occurrence is increased when the worshiper understands what is happening through the order and chooses to make it happen through intention. The consequence of this choice is an intensified spirituality.

Third, restore more frequent celebration of the eucharist. Beginning with the primitive Christian community, the church has always and everywhere recognized that Christ becomes mystically present in his saving and healing power at the eucharist. If this is true, the neglect of a regular eucharistic spirituality is to our own spiritual peril. On the other hand, a regular encounter with Christ at the table is a source of spiritual renewal. Each time we come to the table and stretch forth our hands to receive the bread of heaven and lift our lips to receive the cup of salvation, our vision of life in Christ is reconfirmed. Consequently there is an urgent need among Protestant churches to restore weekly Communion.

Finally, restore the church year. The church year is one of the most important sources available to the Christian for an ongoing spirituality. It not only links Sunday to Sunday, but provides a Christocentric daily spirituality for the worshiper. The neglect of the church year by many Protestants has left us without a significant external order for the annual organization of a spiritual pilgrimage linked with worship. The church year celebrated through a daily devotion marking Advent, Christmas, Epiphany, Lent, Holy Week, Easter, and Pentecost is the Christian way of sanctifying time, thus bringing time under the lordship of Christ. To neglect this Christian marking of time is to succumb to a secular calendar. To restore this Christian concept of time in the church corporate and in individual daily devotion links worship and spirituality in a way that no other discipline can match, for it links every day of life with the story that gives meaning to all of life.

CONCLUSION

In conclusion, let it be said that recovering the relationship between worship and spirituality outlined here is no mere gimmick. It reaches back into a tradition by which a multitude of Christians have lived for centuries. It has staying power. But unless it is vitalized by true faith in Christ living, dying, and rising again for the salvation of the world, it becomes a dead ritual. Ritual is important because it organizes experience. But what we want is a ritual accompanied by faith. This is the kind of ritual that brings depth to our relationship with God, provides us with significant religious experience, and shapes our spirituality.

STUDY GUIDE

*Read Session 8, "Grow in Christ,"
before starting the study guide.*

PART I: PERSONAL STUDY

Complete the following questions individually.

1. *Life Connection*

 ♦ Recall a one-liner that you either thought up or heard from someone
 else—a one-liner that seemed to go to the heart of the matter (any issue).

 _____

 _____

 _____

 _____

 _____

 _____

2. *Content Questions*

 ♦ Summarize in your own words the two basic biblical principles of worship.

 a. _____

 _____

 _____

 b. _____

 _____

 _____

 ♦ In what ways does worship form us spiritually? Explain each in your own
 words.

 a. _____

 _____

 _____

 b. _____

 _____

 _____

◆ Summarize in your own words the four ways worship and spirituality may be brought together.

a. _____

_____

b. _____

_____

c. _____

_____

d. _____

_____

3. *Application*

◆ How does worship shape and form your own spiritual life? _____

_____

_____

_____

_____

_____

_____

PART II: GROUP DISCUSSION

The following questions are designed for group discussion. Share the insights you gained from your personal study in Part I.

Write out all answers that group members give to the questions on a chalkboard, a flip chart, or a dry erase board.

1. *Life Connection*

◆ Begin your discussion by asking people to present the one-liners that have influenced their lives. These one-liners may cover a broad range of topics and do not need to be related to the subject of this session.

◆ Ask people to respond to the one-liner that is the subject of this session: "I want nothing more than that the word of God take up residence in my life and shape me into Christ-likeness."

2. *Thought Questions*

♦ Read 1 Peter 2:9–10. How does this passage express the two basic principles of Christian worship?

♦ Read through Revelation 4–5 and discover how Christ is at the center of worship.

♦ Put the summary of the fourfold pattern of worship in a column on the left side of the board. On the right side of the board put what each part of worship does to order spiritual formation. Discuss your experience (or lack) of this principle.

♦ How does the eucharist shape our spiritual life?

♦ List each season of the Christian year on the left side of the board (Advent, Christmas, Epiphany, Lent, Holy Week, Easter, Pentecost). How does each season shape our spiritual life? Put your answers on the right side of the board.

3. *Application*

♦ Evaluate the relationship between worship and spiritual formation in your church. Exactly how do people feel worship orders their spiritual growth?

♦ Plan a fourfold pattern of worship. As you plan, discuss how the gathering, the word, the table, and the dismissal rehearse a relationship with God and form the spiritual life.

♦ Plan the *themes* for the Christian year and discuss how the theme of each season may affect and shape the spiritual life.

TEACHING THE FAITH

A Study in Worship and Education

 One of the most challenging spiritual events of my life occurred when an Orthodox Rabbi invited me and my wife to a Shabbat (Sabbath) dinner in their home.

This event forced me to think more clearly about the Jewish tradition of education. Jews have successfully integrated worship and education. In order to understand how they have achieved this, we need to go all the way back to a directive given by God to Moses.

God said, "In the future, when your son asks you 'What is the meaning of the stipulations, decrees and laws the LORD our God has commanded you?' tell him: 'We were slaves of Pharaoh in Egypt, but the LORD brought us out of Egypt with a mighty hand' " (Deut 6:20–21).

The Jews, following this directive, have developed worship such as the Shabbat and the Passover to inform and shape the community of faith around God's mighty acts of salvation. The Christian church has not been as successful as the Jews in bringing worship and education together. But, like the Jews, we have a story to tell, a story of how God rescued us from the hand of the evil one and delivered us as God's people. Let's explore this story and discover its relationship to worship and education.

DEFINING CHRISTIAN EDUCATION

Education in general has to do with information, formation, and transformation. Let's look at these three goals of education in terms of the Christian faith:

- The *information* of the Christian faith is the story of the Bible—creation, fall, and redemption. Worship is based on this story because it proclaims it in the word and enacts it in the eucharist.

+ *Formation* in the Christian faith has to do with the development of Christian values, attitudes, and lifestyles.
+ *Transformation* has to do with changed lives, changed families, and changed societies.

Christian education through worship touches on all three of these matters. Let's see how.

WORSHIP AND CHRISTIAN EDUCATION

The question we must address is simply this: how does worship provide us with information that forms our values and transforms our lives?

Robert Pazmiño, a Christian education scholar, suggests that worship educates us in four ways: through proclamation; through the experience of community; through the call to service; and through a challenge to contemporary society. Let's look at all four more closely.

1. Education through proclamation in worship. Worship proclaims the story that is central to the Christian faith, namely the story of humankind's fall from God and God's saving and rescuing work in Jesus. While this is all information about the world, it is information that demands a response.

+ We are not allowed to simply listen to the information and pay no attention to it. We are called to be converted by the person this information presents. Faith in Jesus Christ as Lord and Savior is the initial set of Christian education (see Eph 2:1–10).

2. Education through the experience of community in worship. We learn a considerable amount through the environment in which we live and the models of life that we observe.

+ For this reason educators are always reminding us of the roles we model at home, in the workplace, and at leisure.
+ People say, "I want to be like her." They watch her actions, her walk, her way of dress, her outlook, and then they model themselves after her. This is not only true in the secular world. It is equally true in the Christian world.
+ We learn our values and attitudes and lifestyle from the people we admire most.
+ The Christian church is a community. It is made up of men and women who express values, attitudes, and lifestyles. These may be unspoken as well as spoken. But it is the unspoken model we live that speaks most

loudly and shapes the worshiping community most distinctly (see Acts 2:42–47).

3. Education through the call to service in worship. We have already noted that worship is not only what we do when we gather to rehearse God's saving deed. It is also what we do in all of life (Rom 12:1).

◆ Worship empowers us for service. It educates us to care about the needs and concerns of others. This is precisely the point made by the writer of Hebrews: "Let us consider how we may spur one another on toward love and good deeds. Let us not give up meeting together, as some are in the habit of doing, but let us encourage one another" (Heb 10:24–25).

◆ To know Christ and to follow after him means to be concerned about doing service to the world. We are to care for the poor, the needy, the orphaned, and the distressed (see Jas 1:19–27).

4. Education through challenge to contemporary society. Worship also has a prophetic dimension because it understands and celebrates true Christian values. Then it compares and contrasts these values to the values of the world.

◆ Baptism is a good example. In baptism we say no to the powers of evil and yes to the fruits of the spirit. We die to sin and we are born to a new life (Rom 6:1–14).

◆ The meaning of baptism is proclaimed in preaching. The church is in need of more prophetic preaching—preaching that compares the value of the Christian life with the materialistic and consumer values of society and calls for a lifestyle in keeping with the values of the Christian faith.

CONCLUSION

This study shows us that worship has much to do with educating us into the Christian way of life. Worship deals with information that forms our values and attitudes and sends us forth as transformed people called to transform the world.

STUDY GUIDE

Read Session 9, "Teaching the Faith,"
before starting the study guide.

PART I: PERSONAL STUDY

Complete the following questions individually.

1. *Life Connection*

♦ Stories often make a significant impact on us and educate us in ways that direct information given in command statements sometimes fails to do. A command says "do it this way" while a story gives you a real-life experience. Give an example of a story told to you that taught you something important. _____

_____

_____

_____

2. *Content Questions*

♦ Use your own words to summarize the three goals of education.

a. _____

_____

_____

b. _____

_____

_____

c. _____

_____

_____

♦ List without comment the four ways worship educates.

a. _____

b. _____

c. _____

d. _____

◆ Read Ephesians 2:1–10. How does this passage suggest that the story of faith which worship proclaims is not mere information, but information that converts us and shapes the direction of our lives? Write down every statement in this passage that alludes to information that transforms life.

_____

_____

_____

_____

_____

◆ Read Acts 2:42–47. What values do you find expressed in this worshiping community that have the power to shape the values of individuals within the community? Write them out. _____

_____

_____

_____

_____

_____

◆ Read James 1:19–27. This passage was written to be read in the worshiping communities of the early church. Write down everything from this passage that calls a person to action and Christian service. _____

_____

_____

_____

_____

◆ Read Romans 6:1–14. How does baptism, which is a part of worship, act as a "prophetic no" to false values and a "prophetic yes" to the values of the Christian faith? _____

_____

_____

_____

_____

3. *Application*

• Comment on how worship has educated you toward the Christian way of life. _____

_____

_____

_____

_____

PART II: GROUP DISCUSSION

The following questions are designed for group study. Share the insights you gained from your personal study in Part I.

Write out all answers that group members give to the questions on a chalkboard, a flip chart, or a dry erase board.

1. *Life Connection*

• Begin your discussion by asking members of the group to share a story that taught them an important truth or value.

• Explore how the Christian story educates a person and a community.

2. *Thought Questions*

• Review the three goals of education. How does worship accomplish each goal?

• Review the four ways worship educates. List them on the chalkboard or flip chart (do not go into length because the next questions will do that).

• Read Ephesians 2:1–10 and discuss how this passage presents information that leads to the transformation of life.

• Read Acts 2:42–47 and discuss how community values influence and shape the values of the children and young people particularly.

• Read James 1:19–27 and discuss how reading Scripture and preaching in worship may form our values.

- Read Romans 6:1–14 and discuss how baptism is a prophetic message against the evils in our society.

3. *Application*

- Evaluate the educational impact of your worship by the goals of information, values, and transformation. Does your worship make this kind of impact?

- Evaluate your worship by the four ways worship educates (proclamation, community model, call to service, prophetic challenge).

- Brainstorm on how the worship of your church may better fulfill the goals of worship and education.

PART III

⋙⋘

MINISTRY

FROM THE

WORSHIPING

COMMUNITY

TO OTHERS

WELCOME TO THE FAMILY!

A Study in Worship Hospitality

A few years ago my two daughters were students at Westmont College in Santa Barbara, California. One weekend when I was there visiting them, I decided we should attend an Orthodox church in Golita, St. Athanasius Orthodox Church. I knew of the church because one of my friends, Father Peter Gillquist, was on its staff. I didn't let Father Peter know that we were coming. We just showed up.

As we entered the vestibule, a very friendly person asked us to sign the guest register. I thought this to be unusual, since in most churches visitors sign after the service. The church was packed, but the ushers were able to find us a few seats in the second row. The spirit of the worship was so full of hospitable warmth that my daughter Lexi leaned toward me and said, "Dad, these people love each other. You can feel it." I quite agreed.

In this Orthodox liturgy there is a break in the flow of worship after the service of the word before the celebration of the eucharist. This time is used for announcements. The people were quite joyous during the announcements—laughing over one matter or the other (you don't expect to experience such freedom in a formal liturgical setting). During the announcements every visitor was introduced, including the three of us. Generally, I don't like that kind of thing, but in this setting it worked. We were really made to feel at home.

After the service my daughters and I were greeted by numerous people. To top it all off, Peter Gillquist and two families not known to us at all invited us for lunch. We were impressed!

My daughters both said, "If this were not so far away from the college, I'd make it my church home."

In this study we want to ask how we can make our worship so hospitable that visitors will say, "This is the place for me!"

The Biblical Background

It is interesting that the writings of the early church fathers mention the gift of hospitality more than any of the other gifts.

The New Testament literature suggests that the early Christian churches were characterized by a sense of hospitality.

For example, consider the earliest description of worship in Jerusalem. The text tells us that "they broke bread in their homes and ate together with glad and sincere hearts" (Acts 2:46).

Read Romans 16. Paul devotes an entire chapter of this letter to the Roman people to greeting this and that person. And then he refers to Gaius, his host, and says, "Gaius, whose hospitality I and the whole church here enjoy, sends you his greetings" (Rom 16:23).

When Paul wrote to the Philippian church (the church that some scholars argue was Paul's home church), he writes, "I thank my God every time I remember you" (1:3) and "I have you in my heart" (1:7). These words express the heart of Christian hospitality. Hospitable people!

Hospitable Space

Once we have established a hospitable community of people, we need to make certain that our space is welcoming. Here are some ideas.

- Make certain there is adequate parking space. Visitors who cannot find a place to park will probably not return.
- Create obvious directional signs. First-time visitors need to know which door to enter, where to find the nursery, etc.
- Have an informational center in the narthex. Visitors may want to inquire about the church and its community life. Have an attractive brochure you can give to visitors that introduces the church and gives information about the various study, prayer, fellowship, or social action groups.
- Have plenty of greeters so that one greeter may say more than hello. A greeter may introduce the visitors to others or may simply answer questions. The same greeter may follow up with a phone call or arrange to have coffee and a time of fellowship.
- Be sure to have adequate nursery facilities. A visitor wants to know that a child left in another person's care will receive love and adequate attention.
- Make sure the usher is appropriately friendly.

◆ Make certain that people are seated where they can *see* and *hear.*

These simple considerations make an immediate impact on visitors, many of whom are church-shopping. But remember that these arrangements support good worship, but they can never be a substitute for it.

HOSPITABLE WORSHIP

Because I visit a great many churches I have found that I can actually *feel* the hospitality (or the coldness) of a community of people at worship.

My own experience suggests that the hospitality of worship is expressed in the following:

◆ Fervent singing. A community of people who sing with conviction and enthusiasm expresses a warmth and love toward God that suggests a warmth and love toward each other. Strong singing always requires good instrumental or vocal leadership.

◆ Warm leadership. Worship leaders and ministers need to make sure that they lead with a spirit of genuine sincerity and openness. A leader who appears distracted or disinterested can set a negative worship mood, whereas a person who provides strong, intentional, and warm leadership will set a positive and hospitable mood for worship.

◆ A ritual of welcome or the passing of the peace. Many churches take a moment at the beginning of the service for a rite of welcome. This sets a positive tone for what happens in worship among those present.

An ancient tradition that has made a comeback in renewal worship is the passing of the peace. This ritual may occur at the end of the gathering or at the end of the service of the word. The minister may say, "The Peace of the Lord be with you." The people respond, "And also with you." Then the people greet one another, saying "The peace of the Lord be with you." In this action the church momentarily experiences the shalom of God that will one day rest over the entire created order.

CONCLUSION

Hospitable people. Hospitable space. Hospitable worship! Once I attended a church where the minister said, "Our God is a welcoming God. The only way our visitors will know that God is a welcoming God is if we are a welcoming people." Good spiritual advice!

STUDY GUIDE

Read Session 10, "Welcome to the Family!"
before starting the study guide.

PART I: PERSONAL STUDY

Complete the following questions individually.

1. *Life Connection*
• Recall a church you visited that was unusually warm and hospitable. Give an opposite experience as well. _____

_____

_____

_____

_____

_____

_____

2. *Content Questions*
• Read Acts 2:42–47. What signs of hospitality do you find in this passage?

_____

_____

_____

_____

_____

• Read Romans 16:1–27. List all the evidences of a warm and hospitable community that you can find in this account of the Roman church.

_____

_____

_____

_____

_____

_____

◆ Summarize in your own words the principles that make for a hospitable space.

a. _____
b. _____
c. _____
d. _____
e. _____
f. _____
g. _____

◆ Name at least three ways you can experience hospitality in worship.

◆ a. _____
_____
_____

b. _____
_____
_____

c. _____
_____
_____

3. *Application*

◆ How do you yourself contribute to the experience of hospitality in the worship of your church? _____
_____
_____
_____
_____

PART II: GROUP DISCUSSION

The following questions are designed for group discussion. Share your insights from your personal study in Part I.

Write out all answers that group members give to the questions on a chalkboard, a flip chart, or a dry erase board.

1. *Life Connection*
   - Begin your discussion by asking for examples of hospitable experiences in churches visited. The opposite?

2. *Thought Questions*
   - Review Acts 2:42–47, commenting on the signs of hospitality evident in the Jerusalem community.
   - Review Romans 16:1–27, commenting on the signs of hospitality evident in the Roman church.

3. *Application*
   - List the seven principles of hospitable space on the chalkboard or flip chart on the left side. Evaluate the space of your church by these principles. Place summary comments in a parallel column on the right side.
   - Indicate the three ways hospitality can be expressed in worship on the left side of the chalkboard or flip chart. Discuss how you can improve the hospitality of your worship. Write your comments on the right side of the board.

Go Forth into All the World

A Study in Worship and Evangelism

 The subject of worship and evangelism has become a hot topic in the church in the latter part of the twentieth century.

Willow Creek Community Church, a large and widely known church in the Chicago area, has pioneered the seeker service tradition that separates worship and evangelism. Every member participates in evangelism (and the seeker service assists this process). Worship is for the believer only.

Another contemporary approach to evangelism has been pioneered by the Roman Catholic Church. It is called the RCIA (Rite for the Christian Initiation of Adults). This form of evangelism is adapted from third- and fourth-century practices of worship and evangelism.

Both of these approaches have been widely accepted in the contemporary world. So we will turn to these two approaches to evangelism and worship in order to learn from them the practice of worship and evangelism in the church today.

The Great Commission

Just before Jesus ascended into heaven, he gave his disciples the following commission: "You will receive power when the Holy Spirit comes on you; and you will be my witnesses in Jerusalem, and in all Judea and Samaria, and to the ends of the earth" (Acts 1:8).

This commission turned the Christian faith into a missionary movement. Its calling is to tell others about Christ and convert them to the Christian faith. With this mandate in mind, let's ask how evangelism is being done in the contemporary church.

The Seeker Model of Evangelism

Willow Creek Community Church has pioneered a sevenfold process to bring people to Jesus and the church. Here is a summary of that process.

- Every member evangelism. The assumption behind every member evangelism is the conviction that the Great Commission is meant for *everyone*, not just the clergy or those who are called to be full-time evangelists. Every Christian is to "tell the story" and lead others to faith.
- Learn to give a witness. Because every Christian is to fulfill the Great Commission, everyone must learn how to tell their story to friends. Classes are conducted to train people. People are encouraged to make friends with the unchurched.
- The seeker service. The seeker service is a nonthreatening service for those who are inquiring about the faith. It is not a worship service. It is a program designed to present the Christian faith in a winsome way. The person seeking God ideally comes to the Saturday night or Sunday seeker service with a Christian friend.
- The new covenant community. A person who becomes a Christian is expected to be involved in the worship of the church, which occurs on a midweek evening. This worship consists of weekly singing and Bible teaching and a celebration of the Lord's Supper once a month.
- Small group discipleship. Each new Christian is put into a small group for discipleship in prayer, Bible study, and Christian living.
- Discernment of gifts. Each new Christian is taught to discern his or her spiritual gift and put it to work in the church.
- Stewardship. Each new Christian is taught to be a good steward of all of his or her time and talents, not just money.

This brief survey demonstrates that the seeker tradition is a process whereby a person is nurtured into the Christian faith. It is not a quick drive-by witness, but one that is committed to the long-term journey of faith.

THE RITE FOR THE CHRISTIAN INITIATION OF ADULTS

The Roman Catholic Church, drawing from the practice of the third and fourth centuries, has developed an approach to evangelism that is tied into the worship of the church. It also has seven steps.

- Inquiry. A person may be a visitor at worship or may have been brought to church by a friend. This person, wanting to know more about following Jesus, may enter a special inquiry class designed to introduce the Christian faith.

- The rite of welcome. This ritual of welcoming the person into the fellowship of believers occurs in the morning worship. The converting person is welcomed into the family of God and attends the service of the word, but does not participate in the eucharist.
- The catechumenate. The converting person attends morning worship but is dismissed to a special course of study after the service of the word. While baptized Christians receive the eucharist, the converting person may reflect on the sermon. Other training classes in the Christian life may be taught during the week.
- The rite of election. Having passed through the catechumenate, the converting persons are brought before the congregation for the rite of election. They are asked to choose God, who has chosen them. They respond by writing their names in a book known as the book of life.
- Purification and enlightenment. The converting person now goes through an intense period of spiritual preparation during Lent as a way to get ready for baptism at the great paschal vigil. The emphasis of this time is the warfare Christians have with the powers of evil and the need to overcome through Christ (see Eph 6:12).
- The baptism. The converting person is baptized in the name of the Father, the Son, and the Holy Spirit on Easter Sunday morning. The baptism is part of a larger service known as the great paschal vigil, a service dating from the early church, now revised and updated for the contemporary world.
- Mystagogy. The final period of time for the converting person who is now (during the Easter Season) integrated into the full life of the church and receives the eucharist. The person's gifts are discerned and put to work in the church. The convert is encouraged to live the Christian faith and bring others to Jesus.

This brief summary demonstrates that the RICA is a process evangelism that works within worship to bring persons to Christ. It is a very effective approach to evangelism in many Catholic churches that has resulted in considerable growth in the Catholic community.

CONCLUSION

Both Protestants and Catholics of renewing churches have recognized that evangelism lies at the heart of the Christian faith. Because worship "tells the story," it is the context in which those who seek or inquire can first hear the good news that God in Christ can transform their lives and make them new.

STUDY GUIDE

Read Session 11, "Go Forth into All the World,"
before starting the study guide.

PART I: PERSONAL STUDY

Complete the following questions individually.

1. *Life Connection*

• What has been your experience of the relationship between worship and evangelism in your church (or in another)? _____

_____

_____

_____

_____

_____

_____

_____

_____

_____

2. *Content Questions*

• Most people argue that the Great Commission of Acts 1:8 was given to every Christian, not just those called to be evangelists. Do you agree or disagree? Why? _____

_____

_____

_____

_____

_____

_____

_____

_____

◆ Briefly summarize the seven steps of evangelism at Willow Creek Community Church.

a. Every member evangelism _____

_____

b. Learn to give a witness _____

_____

c. The seeker service _____

_____

d. The new covenant community _____

_____

e. Small group discipleship _____

_____

f. Discernment of gifts _____

_____

g. Stewardship _____

_____

◆ How do these seven steps *process* a person into Christ and the church?

_____

_____

_____

_____

_____

_____

_____

_____

♦ Briefly summarize the seven steps of the Rite for the Christian Initiation of Adults (RCIA) used by the Catholic Church.

a. Inquiry _____

_____

b. Rite of welcome _____

_____

c. The catechumenate _____

_____

d. The rite of election _____

_____

e. Purification and enlightenment _____

_____

f. The baptism _____

_____

g. Mystagogy _____

_____

♦ How do these seven steps *process* a person into Christ and the church?

_____

_____

_____

_____

♦ How would you compare the seven steps at Willow Creek to the seven steps of the RCIA? _____

_____

_____

_____

_____

3. *Application*

♦ Was your conversion into Christ and the church a process? If so, how?

_____

_____

_____

_____

PART II: GROUP DISCUSSION

The following questions are designed for group discussion. Share your insights from your personal study in Part I.

Write out all answers that group members give to the questions on a chalkboard, a flip chart, or a dry erase board.

1. *Life Connection*
- Begin your discussion by asking various class members to comment on their experience of worship and evangelism in this or in other churches.

2. *Thought Questions*
- Review the seven steps of evangelism at Willow Creek Church.
- Review the seven steps of worship and evangelism used by the RCIA.
- Put the seven steps of evangelism from Willow Creek Church on the left side of the chalkboard. Then place the seven steps from the RCIA on the right side. Compare the two. Are there similarities? Are there differences?

3. *Application*
- Evaluate the approach to evangelism used in your church. How does it compare to the Willow Creek model and the RCIA model?
- Which of these two models would work better in your church?
- Brainstorm how the model you have chosen might be put into place.

DOING THE WORD

A Study in Worship and Social Justice

I don't know about you, but every once in a while I have an aha! It may come from something I have read, from something I have heard, or from something that has been brewing within me for some time. But all of a sudden it becomes clear. I had that kind of an aha! when I was reading the early church fathers about the eucharist.

For them the eucharist meant not only the spiritual provision of God caring for us but also the need for the Christian community to care for others.

For example, when the Christians brought bread and wine to the table for the eucharist, they also brought foodstuffs that were placed on the table, blessed, and then given to the poor.

Here is a clear connection between worship and the need to care for others. This was an aha! for me because I had never made the connection between the eucharist as a symbol of God's love directed toward us and our food given to the needy as an outpouring of Eucharistic love.

A BIBLICAL BASIS FOR WORSHIP AND SOCIAL JUSTICE

One of the most familiar passages in Scripture on worship and social justice is found in Amos. Here God says:

> Away with the noise of your songs!
>> I will not listen to the music of your harps.
> But let justice roll on like a river,
>> righteousness like a never-failing stream! (Amos 5:23–24)

God is not saying "I don't want your worship." God is saying, "I don't want worship that is not backed up by a life concerned for others." That kind of worship is hollow and empty. In other words, true worship is, as expressed in the *Book of Common Prayer*, "not only with our lips, but also with our lives."

This prayer is backed up by the concept of the reign of God (the kingdom that is to come) in the New Testament. Jesus has come to inaugurate a new beginning for the world, which will be consummated in the new heavens and the new earth. The message of prayer is "thy kingdom come, thy will be done on earth as it is in heaven." There is a place where God rules and where God's will is done—heaven. The hope of earth is that God's reign of truth and justice will be experienced in the here and now, in our time and in our place. Our worship task is to witness to God's social order by living its reality now.

Jesus' preaching, as exemplified in the Sermon on the Mount, shows that his heart is for the poor, the needy, the destitute (Matt 5:1–12).

ACTS OF WORSHIP AND SOCIAL JUSTICE

Historically the church has always addressed the relationship between worship and social justice in prayers, the sermon, the hymnody, and the eucharistic celebration. Let's look at several examples.

PRAYER

One of the earliest historical prayers of worship comes from the pen of Clement of Rome, a bishop of the late first century. Below is a portion of the bidding prayer that survives from the liturgy used in Rome about AD 96, a prayer that shows a deep concern for social justice. The leader would pray "deliver the oppressed." The people would then add out loud their specific requests. At the end of their prayers the amen would be said followed by the next prayer.

We beg you, Lord, to help and defend us.
Deliver the oppressed. . . . Amen.
Pity the insignificant. . . . Amen.
Raise the fallen. . . . Amen.
Show yourself to the needy. . . . Amen.
Heal the sick. . . . Amen.
Bring back those of your people who have gone astray. . . . Amen.
Feed the hungry. . . . Amen.
Lift up the weak. . . . Amen.
Take off the prisoner's chains. . . . Amen.
May every nation come to know,
that you alone are God,
that Jesus Christ is your child,
that we are your people,
the sheep that you pasture. Amen.

THE SERMON

A document known as the *Didache* (teaching) was circulated in the early church, particularly in the area of Palestine. This document contains an insight into the church's concern for social justice. French scholarship claims that the document may go back to a date as early as AD 50. Others argue it was written around the turn of the century.

Regardless of the date of origin, the document gives us a clear insight into how deeply early Christian worship was committed to social justice in its preaching and teaching. Here is a sample of its teaching:

> Those who persecute good people, who hate truth, who love lies, who are ignorant of the reward of uprightness, who do not "abide by goodness" or justice, and are on the alert not for goodness but for evil: gentleness and patience are remote from them. "They love vanity," "look for profit," have no pity for the poor, do not exert themselves for the oppressed, ignore their Maker, "murder children," corrupt God's image, turn their backs on the needy, oppress the afflicted, defend the rich, unjustly condemn the poor, and are thoroughly wicked. My children, may you be saved from all this! (5.3–6)

THE KISS OF PEACE

An ancient worship custom known as the kiss of peace has been revived in contemporary worship renewal. Paul urges his readers to follow this practice (Rom 16:16; 1 Cor 16:20; 2 Cor 13:12; compare 1 Thess 5:26). Peter also reminds his readers to pass the peace (1 Pet 5:14). It continued as a ritual in the early church and is found in all the ancient liturgies.

What did it mean and how can it be practiced?

The root meaning of the passing of the peace is found in the Old Testament meaning of God's shalom (peace). The hope of Israel is that someday the swords of the world will be turned into plowshares and the peace of God will rule over all God's creation (see Isa 2:4). This is, of course, a Christian concept as well (see Rev 20–22). In worship when we pass the peace of Christ, we momentarily experience the shalom of God and foreshadow the great day of peace to come.

CONCLUSION

Worship is not just what we do when we gather together to hear God's word and celebrate at the table. Public worship empowers our lives in the world and calls us to a life of action that does good for others in the name of Jesus.

STUDY GUIDE

Read Session 12, "Doing the Word,"
before starting the study guide.

PART I: PERSONAL STUDY

Complete the following questions individually.

1. *Life Connection*

♦ Recall a spiritual "aha!" experience that you had at some point in your life. How did it come about? What did you learn or perceive? _____

_____

_____

_____

_____

_____

2. *Content Questions*

♦ Use your own words to explain the connection between the eucharist and the poor in the early Christian tradition of worship. _____

_____

_____

_____

_____

_____

♦ Read Amos 5:23–24. How does this passage speak to worship and social justice? _____

_____

_____

_____

_____

_____

- How do you interpret the phrase "thy kingdom come, thy will be done on earth as it is in heaven" from the Lord's Prayer? How does it relate to worship and social justice? _____

_____

_____

_____

- Read Matthew 5:1–12. How does Jesus' preaching relate to worship and social justice? _____

_____

_____

_____

- Read, study, and reflect on the prayer from Clement of Rome. How does it move you to compassion for the poor and the needy? _____

_____

_____

_____

_____

- Read, study, and reflect on the sermonic instruction from the Didache. How does this material move you to compassion for the poor and needy?

_____

_____

_____

_____

- Explain how the passing of the peace is a prophetic sign of the relationship between worship and social justice. _____

_____

_____

_____

3. *Application*

• Pray the ancient prayer from Clement of Rome and add to each petition those persons or situations of prayer that come to mind.

PART II: GROUP DISCUSSION

The following questions are designed for group discussion. Share the insights you gained from your personal study in Part I.

Write out all answers that group members give to the questions on a chalkboard, a flip chart, or a dry erase board.

1. *Life Connection*

• Begin your discussion by asking various members of the class to relate stories of aha! that have happened in their lives.

• Ask, "Was anything in this lesson an 'aha!'?"

2. *Thought Questions*

• Explain the connection between the eucharist and the poor.

• Discuss Amos 5:23–24. What is God saying through this passage?

• Discuss the Lord's Prayer. How does this prayer call for a link between worship and social justice?

• Read Matthew 5:1–12. How was Jesus' preaching oriented toward social need?

3. *Application*

• Evaluate the worship of your church. How does it direct attention toward worship and social justice?

• Take time to pray the prayer from Clement of Rome. Ask each person present to call to mind and to speak audibly of the persons and situations that come to mind.

• Discuss the admonition of the Didache. How does each sentence speak to a situation in society today?